The Chess Tournament

Written by: Wes Wesley

Illustrated by: Jasmine Lewis

www.wesbooks.com

Copyright © 2017 Wes Wesley.
All rights reserved. No part of this book may be used or reproduced by any means, graphic, electronic, or mechanical, including photocopying, recording, taping or by any information storage retrieval system without the written permission of the author except in the case of brief quotations embodied in critical articles and reviews.
This is a work of fiction. All of the characters, names, incidents, organizations, and dialogue in this novel are either the products of the author's imagination or are used fictitiously.
Because of the dynamic nature of the Internet, any web addresses or links contained in this book may have changed since publication and may no longer be valid.
ISBN:978-1-946903-01-3

To Kristal and Dane, anything is possible – W.W.

Daniel and Rachel are really good friends. Rachel has a big chess tournament coming up in a couple of days. Daniel told Rachel that he would come to her event.

Later that night, Daniel's father was on the phone, and Daniel overheard him say, "Your word is your bond, if you say you are going to do something then do it!"

Daniel didn't know who his father was talking to on the phone but he decided from that day forward that he was always going to keep his promises, starting with Rachel's chess tournament.

Everything was going smoothly until "POP!" Daniel had a flat tire.

Daniel was already running late so he hid his bicycle behind a big tree and decided to walk the rest of the way. He was determined to get there.

As Daniel begin walking a scrappy little dog came up behind him and started biting on his shoe.

The good news is Daniel was able to get his foot out of the shoe, but the bad news is the dog ran in the opposite direction with the shoe in his mouth!

Daniel was committed to going to that chess tournament even though he had a flat tire and was walking on one shoe.

In order for Daniel to get there on time he took a shortcut that required him to climb up, and jump over a fence.

On his way down his pants got caught on the top of the fence and it ripped a hole in them.

Daniel was persistent, nothing could stop him from going to that chess tournament even though he had a flat tire, he was walking on one shoe, and he had a rip in his pants.

Daniel was almost there, he could see the building where Rachel was playing in the chess tournament. The only thing that worried him was the weather.
Rain was starting to fall out of the sky.

Before Daniel could get into the building the rain started pouring down getting Daniel's shirt soaking wet.

So, Daniel had a flat tire...

...he was walking on one shoe...

...had a rip in his pants...

...and his shirt was soaking wet when he finally made it to the chess tournament.

As Daniel walked into the building Rachel immediately came over and asked, "What happened?" Daniel didn't complain, he simply said, "Never mind what happen to me, I just want you to do your best. Now get over there and have some fun."

Rachel ended up winning first place in the whole tournament! The coordinator called her on stage and gave her a big trophy. Daniel was sitting front and center smiling the whole time.

After Rachel received her trophy she came over to Daniel and said, "Thank you for coming, it really means a lot to me!"

Then Daniel said, "No problem, you can trust me. My word is my bond."

www.ingramcontent.com/pod-product-compliance
Lightning Source LLC
Chambersburg PA
CBHW041230040426

42444CB00002B/114